MY FINNISH SOUL

MY FINNISH SOUL

POEMS
AND
PROSE

Kiitos!

GARY V. ANDERSON

Gary V. Anderson

Cover Photo: Steve Ullakko
                    Meeting Hall, Kivijarvi, Finland

Author Photo: Roberta Lang

ISBN 978-0-615-38088-9

Printed in the United States of America
SHELTER BAY PUBLISHING
Bainbridge Island, Washington

This book is
dedicated to the
first Finns.
They took new names,
brought strong backs,
carved out forests,
invented high-lead logging,
hid in valleys,
pulled stumps,
formed co-ops,
yearned.

Contents

I. DEEP RIVER

What events would have you board a sailing ship in Finland, cross the Atlantic, perhaps round the horn, sail up the Pacific coast, over the Columbia River bar to Astoria, Oregon?

1908

One foot in Finland,
the other in America.
A sailing ship,
a promise of white clouds
in a blue sky.
A small wooden box,
contents to begin a new life
in a new world of miners,
loggers and fishermen.

What was she thinking?

*I am the legacy of Maria Eriika Karjalainen,
Jaakko's daughter, born July 15, 1874 in Kuusamo,
Finland and Juho Mykkanen, Emanuel's son, born
June 4, 1869 in Kiuruvesi, Finland. They arrived
separately in 1908 and were known as John and
Maria Manson of Deep River, Washington.*

My Finnish Soul

This poem is about a
Finnish grandfather
arriving on a sailing ship in Astoria,
finding his way to logging camps
on the far shore.

It's about a grandmother
who found her way from Finland
with two children and
cooked in those camps.

This poem is about a Finnish mother,
trapped in servitude and a lifetime of
suolakala and *laksloda*.

It's about poverty, a large family
on a small 40,
living off the land with
smoked sturgeon,
smelt and venison.

This poem is about
growing up in Deep River,
oppressive, long winter rain,
gray leafless alder,
waiting for skunk cabbage to
signal spring.

It's about a drunk father who
logged in his sleep,
shouting *mainline, slack the*

haulback and where is that
God-damned whistle punk.

This poem is about
family violence and
shaping of young minds,
sisu and over the rainbow.
It's about taking more rounds
at home than in war.

• • • •

This poem was written
before I learned
that the bird with the largest eyes
sees the sun first
and will sing earlier.

And before I learned
that a bird with the ability to sing
more than one song
has a greater chance of survival.

And before I learned
that like a tropical songbird,
I prefer the bright light and
long days of summer,
and should migrate with the seasons.

• • • •

Sing, *pikku lintu* sing.
Bird of two worlds
raise your voice,
begin your journey to your
second home.

Rise up in the night.
Look for the stars.
Go find grandfather's
city of skylark.

And when you arrive on
midsummer's eve,
tell me why anyone
would leave Finland.

Pikku mummo was 76 years old. I was 5. She had been in America for 42 years. She spoke no English. It was 1950.

Suolakala

I watch as
pikku mummo
layers the salmon
skin side down.
Rock salt,
fish,
rock salt,
fish.

Ten times.

Then she places a
crockery plate
on top,
followed by a rock,
to hold it all down.

We wait.

She emerges from the
milk house with
one piece of cured
salmon cupped in her apron.

In the kitchen,
unleavened *rieska*
held against her breast,
she draws the knife toward her.

Bread,
unsalted butter,

a slice of salt fish.
Layers of tradition.

I'm always hungry.
Kiitos, little grandma.

John and Maria Manson of Deep River, Washington,
circa 1940s, Finnish grandparents of the author.

There is great value in passing on tools for survival. Our Norwegian grandpa arrived in the summer of 1954 and helped us make it through a rough patch. This poem also illustrates one of the good things about living off the land—we ate nothing but organic food!

The Last Visit

...Loggers all gone fishing
Chainsaws in a pool of cold oil
On back porches of ten thousand
Split-shake houses, quiet in summer rain.

From *The Late Snow & Lumber Strike of the Summer*
of Fifty-Four—Gary Snyder

He complained about
the loggers' strike and
argued unions
with my unemployed father,
down by the woodpile
in the garden,
waiting for the crawfish
to boil in the washtub.

       He said, *come on boys,*
       we have lots to do.
       Grandpa has only
       ten more years to live.

His hands
dripped brine
as he pulled the silver body
of the smelt
from the bucket.
He showed us how to
push the heads
onto nails

sticking through 2x2s,
hanging in the
smokehouse he built
that summer of 1954.

Don't gut the smelt, he said.
Brine 'em and cool smoke over
green alder.
Put 'em in a paper bag
to absorb the oils.
Eat 'em whole.

He crafted a rack behind the barn
and taught us how to
clean the two pickup loads
of illegal sturgeon traded
with the Columbia River
gillnet fisherman for one
case of homebrew.

Let me show you how to do this.
Hang the sturgeon by the tail.
There's no need to gut 'em.
Carefully slice through the skin
in a circle above the tail.
Begin cutting a strip
down the body.
Use pliers to grip the slippery
skin and pull to the head.
Filet without fear boys,
sturgeon have no bones.
Brine 'em and smoke five hours.

Ask your mother to
can 'em in pint
wide mouth Mason jars.

My Finnish grandpa was a logger,
Dad was a logger. I was a logger.
It's difficult
to
romanticize
logging.

The School of Logging

Logging on the slopes of St. Helens,
thanks to the Columbus Day storm of '62.
It took the barn, the chicken coop, then
the log-house sauna.

Now we salvage the
six foot fir and hemlock,
laid flat, giant toothpicks in a row
down those steep hills.

We set chokers on the high-lead,
forty feet of twisted cable,
memory of a coil spring.
Listen for the last of four
Wirkkala choker-bells to click,
go ahead on'er,
screams the rigg'n slinger.
Run boys, run.

We were strong and fast,
teenage loggers.
Flirting with girls and death,
at three fifty an hour.
We lived hard, dirty, and sprained.
Learned to splice cable,
drive a railroad spike, cuss.
All useful logger skills.

25

REFRESHER COURSE 2003

I asked an old timber faller in Poulsbo,
as I was preparing his tax return,
how could they buck those trees
lying face down, roots uphill?
Son, he said in a whisper,
you go to the base of the hill,
find the first stick at the bottom of the pile,
cut that one,
work your way to the top.

II. DEER LAKE

My God lives in the forest. Probably a forest covered in snow. If you spent time listening to sermons delivered by the Finnish Reverend, John Haverinen, in the 1960s at the Naselle Congregational Church, you will recognize the word "ought." That's where I first heard it.

Forester's Prayer

The trees are my cathedral,
Spring-fed brooks my baptismal,
Snowshoes my life raft.

Silence my meditation,
Bluejays my sentinel,
Budding maples the promise.

The spirit guide—my compass—
Helps me go where I ought to go,
Do as I ought to do.

I drew a diagram on the back of an envelope to help a group of hikers find their way to some beautiful trees. Sometimes we take unintended paths.

You Took a Wrong Turn

at the sugar bush,
its rusted sap buckets and copper boiler
scattered on the forest floor.

If you had waded Katy Creek
and walked up the rutted skid trail,
you would have found the
old growth basswood, maple
and yellow birch.

You might have found the
secret room in the sandstone grotto
with its fern-covered walls
and floor of leaves.

Instead, you took the trail to
the crescent of the beaver dam,
around the vernal pond and
into the lost canyon.

I wondered if you heard
the black-throated blue, the mourning warbler
or the hermit thrush in the
dense, damp, lush of the stream bottom.

I wondered if you found a place
where ashes could begin their journey
down those spring-fed brooks,
to Deer Lake, through Superior, to the sea.

This is a familiar tale. Our Finnish mother repeated it often.

Finn Babies

Grandpa was never seen
without his tin pants,
made stiff by spruce pitch
and diesel grease.
Grandma wore layers of
dresses and aprons
and never showed.
You might wonder
how Finnish babies were made,
or where they came from,
until you learned that all
arrived in a black bag,
delivered in the night
by the mid-wife.

Plato believed we should practice dying. I have had a lot of practice. Here is one of the ways.

What I Like to Do Most
(In the Woods)

It could be a limb
in a November blow.
It could be an arrow
from a hunter's bow.
It could be sudden,
or it could be slow,
but when the Reaper
lays me low,
I want to be
pissing in the snow!

This is a poem of yearning. Living in the Upper Peninsula of Michigan was, in hindsight, a privilege and a blessing. As the poem says, being away from family and first friends can be difficult. I know it was too for my Finnish ancestors.

Where is Home?

She calls me a warbler,
with my bright colors in spring
and back to drab in fall.
Warblers—with rainbow
wings in the northwoods,
drab wings in the tropics.
Fledglings in the
forests of Michigan,
winters at the equator.

Where is home?

One foot in the west,
the other in the east.
Brought by adventure and escape,
finding the good life,
happiness beyond expectation,
making a difference,
leaving a legacy,
yearning for family,
first friends.

Where is home?

III. BAINBRIDGE ISLAND

For sons and dogs, I can only hope there is redemption.

Daddy's Home

A man told me,
I tell young women to watch
their boyfriends' care of a dog.
It's a clue to what fathers they'll be.

I wondered if he was talking
about the dog rescued from the roadside
or the one puppy chosen from ten
born under the house,
or the other nine placed
in a burlap bag with rocks?

Or, perhaps,
he meant the four puppies
delivered to the orphanage in Nha Trang.
When we checked on their welfare,
the Nun said,
They tasted just fine.

I believe he was talking about
the black Cocker Spaniel that
cared for me as I worried over my son.
When I held her in my arms,
as she took her last breaths,
I whispered her favorite words,
Daddy's home!

*It has been said that an assertive Finn will stare at **your** shoes. This poem is about outcomes that will never happen. I just needed a metaphor that would allow me to say it.*

My Neighbor Has Tourette's

I watch with envy as he stands
on the sidewalk screaming obscenities.
I want to join in when he grabs his chainsaw,
revs up the engine and swings it full throttle at
low branches of a pine tree,
then picks up his ax and splits wood
to the violent rhythm of one nasty
swear word after another.

But it's the dog I'm worried about.

His master never says,
what a good dog
or *you're so handsome*
or *you're a very smart dog.*
Wagging his tail, the dog
only hears the obscenities,
the chainsaw, and the sound of
splitting wood.

I'm thinking that when his master
is on his death bed
and the dog makes a sudden move or
disturbs the silence in that room—
his master's last words might be,
can't you ever do anything right?

Yesterday, I imagined
I had Tourette's,
screaming,
stop the fucking war,
end the insanity of violence,

give back our country, and

bring back my father so I can tell him
I love him – for the first time.

Author (left) and brother Dan Anderson (right) with
Finnish grandmother, Maria Manson, circa 1950.

Brothers weren't supposed to serve in Vietnam together. I wish mine had not.

From Nha Trang to Da Nang

My brother said,
Nice to see you, but
why're you here?

> *Your dad asked*
> *me to look in on you.*

He's your dad too.

> *Right - but he doesn't*
> *worry about me.*
> *He worries about you.*

Nothing changes
Tell him I've been busy.

> *Were you in this foxhole*
> *during Tet?*

Yes it was my home away from home.
Don't jump down there. It's full
of piss and spent rounds.
You?

> *We're here talk'n, aren't we?*
> *Where's everyone going?*

Tets over.
We are having a barbeque,

47

maybe a baseball game.
Wanna beer?

EARLY FEBRUARY 2010

After your three tours
and forty-two years,
you ask me,

how's it going for you?

> *Tet's not over.*
> I replied.

Waiting for Change

During the Tang Dynasty
in 750 AD,
Chinese poet Du Fu wrote
in *Song of the War Carts,*
...boys seem born to die in foreign weeds.

'Nuf said.

This is for the new soldiers coming home from the new wars, with damaged bodies and jumbled minds.

Veteran's Day

Stone cold Washington, D.C.,
two decades of hurry up and wait.
Smooth black marble,
chiseled names,
guarded by bronze eyes
eternally at the ready.

I wonder why my name
is not on the wall. I ask
when will I believe again?
Will I always feel the
helplessness
of a world gone mad and
the insanity of war?

Back home,
the angel of death
appears at my bedside.
I walk the perimeter,
survey the world through
parted night curtains,
memories that haunt,
return and remind.

Memorial for the dead,
Memorial for the living.
Memorial to return its gaze
and recognize
me in its shiny black face.

And I wonder:
Is dying for your country really the
ultimate sacrifice?

IV. NASELLE

The last best days were days of innocence—for the environment and for our lives. Marie was expected to have dinner on the table when Archie arrived home from work. She had other interests.

Eulogy

For Marie, the best damned fisherwoman a dozer operator could have hoped to know.

Those were the last best days.

Diesel smoke and mineral soil,
the good earth smells of logging
on the upper Naselle.

Down stream,
the uneven ground of the riverbank
welcomed the fresh-caught steelhead,
an *oki-drifter* hanging from its mouth.

One more cast before the cat skinner comes home.

Another

Another

My Finnish Soul would not be complete without a recipe for suolakala and pickled fish. Dorothy Penttila said, "Harte would have been proud to have his recipe published again, especially in a book of poetry."

Adapted from *The Country Cousins' Cookbook, Anderson-Matta-Owens Family Reunion, August 15, 1987,* Harte Penttila, by permission from Dorothy Penttila.

Finnish Pickled Salmon

The quality of pickled salmon depends largely on the quality of fish used. Spring Chinook, with its high fat content, makes the very best pickled salmon, but fall Chinook, Coho and Steelhead trout also make good pickled fish.

Suolakala:

Clean your fish in the usual manner. Cut the fillets away from the back bone, leaving the skin on the fillets. Cut fillets into pieces of about one pound each, or make them larger if you are using a salting crock or large jar. My favorite jar is a three gallon square "battery jar" that I bought at an auction. NEVER use any kind of a metal can or bucket to salt fish.

Fine salt (not iodized) can be used, but I prefer rock salt. Place a layer of salt about ¼ inch deep at the bottom of the jar, top with a layer of fish, skin side down, and alternate layers of fish and salt until the jar is almost full. Cover the top layer of fish with another ¼-inch of salt and place a small flat plate or saucer over it. Place a weight on the plate to hold the fish under the brine.

A brine will form and gradually rise in the jar, but this is a slow process. I prefer to mix a saturated brine and pour it over the salted fish, making sure that it comes well over the top layer of fish.

Cover the jar with a non-metallic lid, or plastic wrap with a wooden cover over it. Store in a cool place.

Pickled Salmon from Suolakala:

After the fish has been in the salt for 10 days, remove a piece or several pieces from the brine, rinse the salt off and drain. Place it skin-side down on a flat cutting board. Using a very sharp knife, remove the skin and cut slices cross-grain, about ¼ inch thick. Place slices in a large bowl, cover with cold water, and let them soak for about four hours to dilute the salt. Taste preference is the best guide to how much salt should be removed. Drain the fish. Slice one medium onion (more if you are making a bigger batch), separate the onion rings and spread over the fish. Add a tablespoon of mixed pickling spice (for a quart-sized batch). Gently mix fish, onions and spices.

Mix a half-and-half solution of vinegar and cold water, using either cider vinegar or distilled white vinegar, and a tablespoon of sugar. Pour this over the fish, making sure there is enough to cover it.

Place in refrigerator or other cool place for at least one day, after which it will be ready to eat. It will keep for well over a week if it stays cool. The pickled onion rings are also tasty.

Except for a persistent feeling of youthful virility and a dense growth of hair on my chest after having eaten Finnish pickled salmon for 50 years, I have noticed no serious after-effects.

Acknowledgements

"1908", "My Finnish Soul", and "Suolakala" were previously published in *Kippis! A Literary Journal of the Finnish North American Literature Association.*

"You Took a Wrong Turn" was selected for *Poetry Corners* by the Bainbridge Island Arts and Humanities Council.

I would like to thank John Willson, a fine poet, mentor and friend, David Stallings, and Kris Hotchkiss, from the Bainbridge Island Poetry Workshop on Strawberry Hill for their kind guidance.

Thanks to Jani Kattilakoski, Jyväskylä, Finland for his help with the Finnish language and Sue Cook for her masterful editorial assistance.

Especially to Roberta Lang for unending support and encouragement.

Glossary of Finnish Words

suolakala—salt fish

laksloda—a casserole, made with layers of *suolakala*, potato and onions

sisu—inner strength

pikku lintu—little bird

Kiuruvesi—city of skylark

pikku mummo—little grandma

rieska—bread made of rye flour, usually unleavened

Author

Gary V. Anderson has been the moderator for the spoken word events at Finnish American Folk Festivals in Naselle, Washington and FinnFest USA in Astoria, Oregon. He writes about growing up Finn, man's relationship with the natural environment and the ironies when looking back over more than 60 years. Although he has been a lifelong resident of the Pacific Northwest, much of his inspiration comes from The Upper Peninsula of Michigan where he lived for ten years.

Order Form

MY FINNISH SOUL

Please send a check or money order
for $15.00 which includes shipping, handling
and sales tax to:

SHELTER BAY PUBLISHING
713 Madison Ave N.
Bainbridge Island, Washington 98110

Or go to :
www.garyandersonpoetry.com

Made in the USA
Charleston, SC
10 August 2010